FLORIDA MAN

SHAWN D. GARNER

To all the Florida men, past, present, and future,
without whom this book would not be possible.

Florida Man
by Shawn D. Garner

This book is for entertainment purposes only. The compilations presented are summaries of published news reports. No warranty is made regarding the accuracy of any information contained within this book.

Cover and Illustrations by Robert Caswell

ISBN-13: 978-0692818022
ISBN-10: 0692818022

With antics becoming more bizarre by the year, Florida Man has become one of social media's most self-deprecating and notorious caricatures of the Sunshine State. Whether calling 911 to report an empty bottle of vodka, stealing a Capri Sun to rehydrate during a police chase, or assaulting his boss with frozen hamburger patties, his reputation seems well deserved. As he casts his social shackles, Florida Man's outlandish behavior and knack for unintelligible decision making have knocked down the boundaries of criminality and typical human decency. We invite you to take a journey with us into the darkest realms of delinquency, that could only occur in Florida.

Crack-Smoking Florida Man Drinks Capri Sun to Rehydrate During Police Chase

Suspect takes a break to rehydrate, stealing Capri Sun pouches

PALM BEACH - A Florida man jumped in his car and sped away after police showed up at his home to execute a search warrant. He peeled out through his back yard and through neighbors chain link fences, continuing to flee on foot after crashing his car. A neighborhood wide police chase involving helicopters, a K9 unit, and several additional officers ensued.

The suspect stopped to rest in an unoccupied house down the street. He changed into a clean shirt he found in the residence and filled several bags with jewelry and other valuables he found in the home. Before continuing to flee, he took three Capri Sun juice pouches out of the refrigerator and drank them, discarding them on the back porch.

He was thirsty, he later told deputies, because he had smoked crack cocaine all day.

As the chase continued, the suspect continued hopping fences, leaving behind a trail of jewelry from his bag. He then broke into another home and asked the homeowner for a glass of water. The homeowner tipped off police, and nearly two-and-a-half hours after the chase began, the suspect was apprehended. While in the police car, he was caught trying to use a paper clip with a bent tip similar to a handcuff key to free himself. Before going to the Palm Beach County Jail, he had to be transported to the hospital to be treated for dehydration, deputies said.

Florida Man Throws Alligator Into Wendy's Drive-Thru Window

Suspect banned from Wendy's, contact with all animals except family dog

JUPITER - A Florida man apologized for throwing a live alligator through the drive-thru window of a Wendy's restaurant, calling it a "stupid prank."

The 24-year-old Jupiter resident was seen on surveillance video paying for an order around 1:30 AM, then tossing a 3.5 foot alligator through the drive-thru window before making a quick getaway. When the cashier realized what the object was, she moved to the edge of the window before hurling herself out.

The suspect was charged with assault with a deadly weapon, illegal possession of an alligator, and petty theft.

Standing before the judge, the man said he "was sorry for what he did ... was just being stupid and not thinking."

"We're just like outdoors kinda people and just anything we find we kinda just like catch... And we just saw an alligator and caught it, ideas start popping and one thing led to another."

But the Palm Beach County Judge was not impressed, calling it one of the most bizarre cases in his 25 years on the bench, and perhaps his final one as he nears retirement. In addition to a fine, and community service, the man was banned from all Wendy's restaurants as well as contact with any animals except a current family dog.

Florida Man Arrested for Dialing 911 When He Wanted Vodka

Suspect with emergency need to keep his buzz going, regrets drunk dial.

NAPLES - A 51-year-old Florida man says he called 911 after becoming upset his girlfriend would not buy him more vodka.

Faking an emergency, the man told dispatchers that his neighbors were fighting, but when deputies arrived at the scene, there was no emergency. According to the police report, the suspect was drunk and angry after his girlfriend would not buy him vodka, so he decided to call 911.

"It's not what I'd call a true emergency, but it's the same bull***t," the suspect told police.

After spending more than an hour at the scene, deputies arrested the man and charged him with a misdemeanor of misusing 911.

Florida Man Found with Active Meth Lab in Pants

Is that a meth lab in your pants or are you just happy to see me?

WALTON COUNTY - A Florida man was arrested after deputies found an active meth lab in his pants leg.

Deputies responded to an anonymous call stating the suspect was in possession of methamphetamine. During their investigation, they discovered an active "One-Pot" meth lab in the pants leg of the 23-year-old resident of Defuniak Springs.

The man was transported to the Walton County Jail. He was charged with manufacturing and trafficking in methamphetamine, and is and is being held on a $25,000 bond.

Florida Man Arrested for Assaulting Krystal Manager With Frozen Hamburger Patties

Suspect faced disciplinary actions for tardiness, prompting outrage

LAKE CITY - A Krystal employee began throwing frozen hamburger patties at his boss after learning he would be reprimanded for tardiness. Lake City Police said the 29-year-old man threw frozen hamburger patties at his boss, then started knocking over equipment and poured cooking oil on the floor of the restaurant. According to the arrest report, the suspect "flipped the circuit breakers, overturned trash cans, and damaged electronic equipment." He tried to flee the scene in his car, but two customers blocked the exit.

The man spat in the face of one of the customers before being successfully restrained by them until police arrived. During questioning by the officers, the suspect again attempted to flee, this time on foot.

He was apprehended and charged with aggravated battery, assault, criminal mischief, resisting an officer without violence, and driving with a suspended license.

Florida Man Calls 911 to Complain About Traffic Ticket

COLLIER COUNTY - A 29-year-old Florida man was pulled over by police for running a stop sign at Boston Avenue and 9th Street. The man denied the infraction, which was witnessed by the officer, and an argument ensued. While the deputy was calling in the suspects information and writing the citation, the suspect called 911 to complain about the delay in writing the ticket. The deputy acknowledged there was a delay, but arrested the man for misuse of 911. The suspect admitted calling 911, and was released after posting a $2000 bond.

Florida Men Surprised to Learn Mannequin is Actually Dead Body

SPRING HILL — Two men hired to clean out a vacant Tampa Bay area house found what they believed to be a mannequin in the garage. They transported it to the local dump, where landfill workers realized it was actually a human body. The hired men thought it was a "Halloween hoax," and continued hauling trash, alerting landfill workers that something was suspicious.

The landfill workers called authorities, who said the deceased man mistaken for a mannequin was a 33-year-old local man who had committed suicide several weeks prior. His body was in an advanced state of decomposition.

The men, as well as the property owner, were released after questioning.

An investigation continues.

Florida Man Proposes to Girlfriend, Ties Ring to Alligator

Bride-to-be calls unique proposal the "greatest surprise of her life"

ORLANDO — A Florida man proposed to his Cleveland girlfriend on a trip to Gatorland in Orlando ... with a little help from an alligator.

As seen on a YouTube video, the unsuspecting girlfriend was brought on stage blindfolded to participate in an "Up Close Encounter" during the Orlando show. After her blindfold was removed, she saw the aspiring groom on one knee, with an engagement ring tied to a baby alligator. The woman, who reportedly loves alligators, embraced the baby alligator in her arms while nodding yes.

"I was secretly more excited to hold the baby alligator than the ring!" she told reporters.

As the show continued, an enormous spider was placed on her hand, and then on top of her new ring. The bride-to-be was not afraid at all, calling it "the greatest surprise of her life."

The two plan to marry later this year in Cleveland.

Man Escapes on Lawn Mower From Intoxicated, Machete-Wielding Florida Man

A man doing yard work narrowly escapes attack on riding lawn mower

PALM BEACH - A resident of Delray Beach narrowly escaped an intoxicated, machete-wielding man by riding off on a lawnmower, according to a report.

The local man, who was doing yard work at the time, told police that the suspect motioned for him to come closer. When he made his way over on a riding lawn mower, the suspect pulled a machete from his pants and pursued him on foot. The alleged attacker then tried getting on a bike to continue the pursuit, but fell off because he was too intoxicated.

Deputies later found the 27-year-old suspect hiding at his residence wearing only his underwear. He became uncooperative with police, and was booked in the Palm Beach County Jail without bail on charges of aggravated assault with a deadly weapon and resisting an officer.

Florida Man Leaving Strip Club Falls Out of Truck, Runs Himself Over

ORLANDO - A 28-year-old Florida man was allegedly leaving a strip club when he fell out of his truck and ran over his own legs, local media report.

According to police, the incident happened around 2:15 A.M. The driverless truck continued down the highway and crashed into a house. The Florida Highway Patrol says the suspect left his I.D. at the strip club before leaving with a group of friends. An arrest warrant has been issued.

Florida Man Rescued from Vending Machine

JACKSONVILLE - A Florida man was rescued from a vending machine on the Westside in Jacksonville, according to authorities. He was found after a caller reported an industrial accident at a packaging company. Authorities would not comment on how the man became entangled in the machine, or how he was rescued. The extent of his injuries are unknown.

Florida Man Removes Facial Tattoos with Welding Grinder

"Drastic action" deemed necessary when conventional treatments failed

CLEARWATER — A Florida man who rehabilitated from gang associations and multiple arrests had his facial tattoos removed with a welding tool.

His first encounter with law enforcement was at age 12 for stealing a golf cart. In the years that followed, the troubled teen tattooed himself with crude methods such as melting checkers and creating a mixture with grease, toothpaste and pencil lead to create tattoo ink. Before long, he had several homegrown tattoos on his face, chest, and arms.

The 22-year-old Clearwater resident realized the gang tattoos on his face would make it difficult to get a job. When standard laser therapy failed to provide a durable result, the man decided drastic action was necessary.

He was finishing a two-year welding course when he hatched the idea to remove them with a welding tool. According to news outlets, he drank 18 beers and rum while his friend went to work with his welding kit. The process removed several layers of skin, including the tattoo, and caused temporary damage to his eye.

Pending criminal charges were dropped.

Florida Man Impersonating Police Pulls Over Detective

Friends, family members duped; but not two off-duty detectives

LEE COUNTY — A 69-year-old Florida man was arrested and charged with falsely impersonating an officer and unlawfully using police insignia after he allegedly tried to pull over a pair of detectives.

He was driving a white Ford Crown Victoria with strobe lights and other markings consistent with a patrol vehicle, according to the incident report. The off-duty detectives in an unmarked vehicle were pursued by the suspect, who then activated the strobe lights to initiate a traffic stop. After the detectives pulled over, the impersonator continued into a supermarket parking lot. The detectives followed the man after realizing the vehicle was not actually law enforcement.

When the suspect was unable to provide proper identification, they detained him until local authorities arrived on the scene.

The suspect's family told police that he had used the vehicle and lights to assist law enforcement with traffic stops in the past. Arrest records, however, show the man has been charged in the past for police impersonation, but described this incident as "a senior moment." The vehicle was impounded pending an investigation.

Florida Man Advertising "Legit Counterfeit $$" on Craigslist Arrested

The shrewd businessman ran a counterfeiting operation out of family's Merritt Island home

BREVARD COUNTY — When a 20-year-old counterfeiter fell on hard times, he took to Craigslist to sell his goods. According to news outlets, Crimeline received an anonymous tip about a person advertising "Legit Counterfeit $$" on Craigslist. "Serious customers only contact me," he added, stating that he'd wouldn't accept anything smaller than $1,500 for $5,000 for fake bills. Undercover detectives replied to the ad, making several purchases of the counterfeit money during a several month investigation, which was assisted by the Secret Service.

According to police, when authorities showed up at the man's house, he said, "I'm going to go ahead and make it easy on you guys. The printer is in my bedroom."

A search recovered a printer, computer, and counterfeit currency. He reportedly used the printer to create $20,000 in fake twenty dollar bills over several months. Court documents show the suspect also sold undercover agents black tar heroin. He faces a possible 20-year sentence in federal prison.

Florida Man Calls 911 Three Times to Ask Dispatcher Out

Suspect, who asked dispatcher if she was "into handcuffs," was later handcuffed by police and arrested

NAPLES — A 45-year-old Florida man called 911 three times, distracting an emergency dispatcher for over six minutes to ask her out.

The intoxicated man said he was "looking for a date or escort service to help him pass the time." During the 6 minute conversation, the man opened up about his alcohol problems and recent stint in rehab, as he reportedly slurred his words and rambled incoherently. He ended the call by asking the woman if she was "into handcuffs," before laughing and hanging up the phone.

Florida Woman Calls 911 to Report Drunk People at Bar

Woman later claims she was concerned about bar patrons driving home intoxicated

MIAMI — A local woman called 911 six times to report that "people were drunk at a bar." She requested that police arrest everyone inside a local bar, later claiming in court that she was concerned about patrons driving home intoxicated. The woman was arrested for abusing 911 services, as well as possession of hydrocodone which was found during a search. The judge astutely observed, "I have a feeling that the mixture between the bar and the hydrocodone probably led to ... the calling of the 911."

Florida Man Arrested After Urination Incident at Thanksgiving

Florida Man Urinates on Cops Sandwich After Arrest

ST. PETERSBURG — A Florida man was arrested after urinating on the living room floor during a Thanksgiving gathering of his girlfriend's family.

According to police, the family members gathered for a Thanksgiving meal, and at some point the 41-year-old suspect excused himself and urinated on the living room floor. His motives are not clear. He was escorted out of the house by his girlfriend's brother-in-law, given $40 and told to find a hotel room. The man became belligerent, shouting obscenities both at his girlfriend's family and at authorities who arrived shortly after the incident. He was arrested and charged with resisting law enforcement and public intoxication.

LEE COUNTY — An 18-year-old Lee County resident was arrested after police were alerted to an early morning disturbance. During his detainment in the squad car, the suspect became unruly, screaming and banging his head against the window.

When the officer asked him to stop, the teen replied, "I will piss in your car!"

Shortly thereafter, the man managed to urinate through the cage into the front seat onto several of the cops' personal items, including a cell phone and one officer's lunch bag. He was transported to Lee County jail on charges of resisting an officer.

Florida Man Pocket-Dials 911 While Operating Meth Lab in Backyard Shed

Police operator listened on the line for thirty minutes after accidental call

DELTONA — Three men are facing charges of illegally manufacturing narcotics after one of the suspects pocked-dialed 911. An operator stayed on the line for over thirty minutes listening to their conversation about manufacturing and selling methamphetamine, according to a police report. One of the men who identified himself as "Tommy" stated that he was on probation and complained that a police official "had been watching him." The sounds of pots and cooking noises could also be heard in the background.

Police traced the call to a backyard shed just north of Orlando. When officers arrived, they looked through an open window to observe a smoking bottle, stoves, and white smoke rising from the shed.

They raided the shed and found "all of the makings of an active meth lab, including coffee filters, a butane torch, batteries, drain opener, plastic tubing, hypodermic needles, lithium strips, lighter fluid, plastic bags and numerous plastic bottles containing a white substance." The trio was arrested and taken into custody. It is not known which of the men was responsible for the pocket-dial.

Florida Inmate Escapes To Buy Beer And Sneaks Back Into Prison

Incident was unnoticed by deputies until suspect fessed up after another escape

PASCO COUNTY — A inmate at the Sumter Correctional Institute was charged with an escape from work detail that went undetected until the man fessed up after a subsequent arrest.

The 27-year-old Florida man revealed the escape to deputies after a later arrest in an attempt to flee law enforcement. The man told deputies that he escaped a work detail a month prior and went to a local food mart with plans to smuggle chewing tobacco, cigarettes, and alcohol back into jail. Video footage showed the man changed clothes before making his purchases, then changed back into his inmate attire and returned to his work crew without anyone noticing.

"It's pretty scary the fact that he's out there in our community just shopping," the local sheriff said.

An investigation into other unauthorized trips as well as whether or not contraband was successfully smuggled into the corrections facility is underway.

In another escape attempt, the same man escaped from a work detail and was found the next day riding his bicycle when he was noticed by police. He is currently serving a six-year sentence for grand theft, burglary, fleeing an officer and drug-related convictions.

The incident prompted deputies to announce periodic unannounced inspections, and the correctional officer in charge of the work projects resigned.

Florida Man Attacks Mailman, Throws Furniture at Truck Over No Mail

Postal carrier tried explaining that the reason he did not receive any mail was because there was none for him

OCALA — A Florida man is under arrest after authorities say he hit a postal carrier and threw furniture at his truck because he didn't have any mail for him.

The 27-year-old suspect is charged with burglary, battery, and criminal mischief. The mailman told police that the suspect approached his vehicle and asked for his mail. When he told him that there was no mail, the man became belligerent, hitting him with an open fist and hurling furniture at his postal truck. The postal carrier said he tried explaining, to no avail, that the reason he did not receive any mail was because there was none for him.

His account was corroborated by a witness at the scene, who states she saw the suspect hitting the mailman and later throwing what appeared to be a broken chair or stool at the vehicle.

Court records show the suspect has been detained for mental health evaluations under the Baker Act twice in the past.

Florida Man Covered Face in Ashes, Stole Car, Then Crashed It

Thief claimed to be a 400-year-old Indian, covered face in ashes, wished onlookers happy new year before driving off

NAPLES — Deputies arrested a Naples man Thursday after witnesses say he stole a woman's car from her driveway then crashed it.

According to a police report, the victim left her car running in her her driveway, and went inside to grab her lunch. When she returned, the Buick was missing from her driveway, prompting her to notify police.

Witnesses at the scene say the 52-year-old Florida man ran through the victims yard claiming he was a 400-year-old Indian. He then jumped into her pool and sat in her fire pit, rubbing ash on his face. Finally, he jumped into the woman's car, wished everyone a happy new year before speeding off.

Police recovered the car after the suspect crashed it near the woman's home. He fled on foot and was apprehended while swimming in a nearby lake. The suspect faces charges of grand theft auto.

Florida Woman Shot by Oven While Trying to Cook Waffles

Woman shot by friend's oven, unaware of .45 caliber magazine stored inside

ST. PETERSBURG — An 18-year-old Florida woman sustained minor injuries when she was shot by a friend's oven, authorities say.

The woman was visiting a friend when the two decided they wanted to make waffles for a late night snack. She turned the oven on, unaware the her friend had stored a magazine containing .45 caliber rounds from his Glock 21 firearm in the oven.

The magazine exploded as the oven heated, causing a rapid fire of bullets which struck the woman. She was treated at a local hospital after removing some of the fragments from her chest and leg.

Investigators say there was extensive damage to the oven as well, likely caused by shell casings.

The woman's injuries were not life threatening. Her friend was not charged because he had a proper concealed weapons permit.

Florida Man Lands Gyrocopter on Capitol Lawn, Demands Finance Reform

Pilot wearing a postal uniform intended to deliver mail and make a statement on campaign finance reform

WASHINGTON, DC — A small gyrocopter with one occupant landed on the West Lawn of the Capitol in Washington, DC. Witnesses report seeing police detain the pilot without incident. The immediate area was closed off while bomb squad investigators cleared the aircraft, and moved it to a secure location. President Obama was in another state at the time.

The pilot, a 61-year-old mailman, had concocted this plan over two years ago, and was proud to have thought out every detail. His plan: to land the ultralight gyrocopter on the lawn of the United States Capitol building, deliver the mail and make a statement on campaign finance reform.

"No sane person would do what I'm doing," he said, adding that he was prepared for the possibility of being shot down.

The FAA reported that the man departed from nearby Gettysburg, Pa., that morning, flying through highly restricted airspace. He was not in contact with them during the flight. Witnesses described a light aircraft with US Postal Service Insignia. The pilot, they say, was wearing a postal uniform and gave a thumbs-up to onlookers shortly before landing.

Florida Man Bitten By Snake That Friends Say He Enjoyed Kissing

Florida Man Takes $4,000 Worth of Chicken and Ribs From Restaurant

TAMPA — A Florida teenager is in critical condition after being bitten in the face by a cottonmouth. The 18-year-old reportedly became attached to the cottonmouth and kept it as a pet. He later told authorities he was trying to kiss the snake before it bit him. Family members killed the snake and brought the boy to a local hospital.

"He kisses it right on the head. Right on the mouth. He's not afraid of death," said a friend.

The Florida teen was proud of the fact that he had kissed the snake 12 times without incident. But on the 13th attempt the snake bit him in the face. Authorities are investigating because he did not have a permit for the dangerous animal.

JACKSONVILLE — A manhunt is underway in Jacksonville for a barbecue bandit who stole $4,000 worth of chicken, ribs, fries and wings from a local barbecue restaurant. He also stole an empty cash register. Authorities say the man was wearing a sweatshirt with "Hilfiger" emblazoned across it in large capital letters. His whereabouts are unknown.

Florida Man Steals Clothes, Bites Security Guard, Flees in Gold Convertible

Suspect later arrested on possession of drug paraphernalia, denies incident took place

COLLIER COUNTY — A Florida man is accused of biting and swinging a knife at a loss prevention officer who confronted him after some clothing was stolen from a department store. The 49-year-old suspect faces criminal charges in connection with the incident.

According to police, the store's manager witnessed the man walk into a dressing room with some merchandise. When he exited without the clothing, the manager confronted him and notified the loss prevention officer. The man resisted their efforts to detain him, biting the loss prevention officer's arm, and assaulting the store manager.

He then began wielding a knife at the two men. When the men backed away, the suspect fled in a gold convertible. He was later arrested on possession of drug paraphernalia, and when confronted with the loss prevention officer's account of the theft, claimed he was trying to return the merchandise, not steal it.

Florida Man Steals More Than 70 Guns, Flees on 3-Wheel Bicycle

"Spider Man" bandit cut hole in ceiling to execute heist, cut arm and fled on three-wheel bicycle

ORLANDO — Sometime after midnight, a burglar ripped a hole in the ceiling of a local Army Navy store and emerged with two bags filled with more than 70 guns. The thief reportedly rappelled down a rope into an area of the store the was without motion detectors or alarms.

"It must be Spider Man," gun-shop owner said of the cat burglar.

Later that evening, the suspect was seen in dark clothing and pedaling a heavily loaded three-wheel bicycle. He disappeared behind a residence, but left behind the bicycle and bags filled with guns. The bags also contained spray can bottles and a crowbar.

He was later found by deputies bleeding from an arm wound, and was taken into custody.

An initial inspection of the gun store did not show any signs of a break in, until authorities discovered a hole in the ceiling, a broken pipe used to gain access to the roof, and several shattered display cases that contained the stolen firearms. They also found black spray paint on the floor, supposedly sprayed by the bandit in an attempt to cover blood from a wound he sustained during the heist.

The 19-year-old suspect was charged with armed burglary of a structure with a firearm, third-degree grand theft of a firearm, possession of a firearm by a convicted felon and criminal mischief. This was his fifth arrest.

Florida Man High on Drugs Rams Car into Jail to 'Visit Friends'

Suspect under the influence of flakka, also known as the "zombie drug"

INDIAN RIVER — A Florida man high on flakka rammed his Toyota through the front doors of a building at the Indian River County Jail, the local sheriff's office reports. He then smashed into a fence and was apprehended after becoming stuck in the razor wire, spitting on a deputy in the process. In a statement to police, the 24-year-old admitted to being high on flakka, and wanted to visit friends who were imprisoned. A deputy on duty at the jail narrowly escaped injury during the crash.

Flakka, also known as the "zombie drug," is related to bath salts, and is known to cause hallucinations, paranoia and psychosis.

The suspect was charged with aggravated assault on a law enforcement officer, battery on a law enforcement officer, three counts of felony criminal mischief, leaving the scene of a crash with property damage and driving under the influence.

Florida Man Sets Up Fake Office to Steal Peoples' Identities, Urine

TALLAHASSEE — A Pensacola man was arrested after authorities say he created a fake online job ad, then stole applicants' identities and their urine.

The 19-year-old suspect posted a fake ad online claiming to hire 1,100 people for various positions. He set up a temporary office in Tallahassee, and obtained applicants' social security numbers and their urine for the fake jobs. He also collected their bank account information, and charged a $25 fee.

He was charged with criminal use of personal identification information and organized communications fraud.

Florida Man Trying to Time Travel Crashes Car Into Businesses

PENSACOLA — A Florida man attempting time travel plowed his vehicle into three businesses, police report. The suspect crashed his Dodge Challenger into a tax services business and adjoining suites. The damage was so extensive that the businesses were forced to close and move to temporary locations while repairs could be made. In a statement to police, the man said he was trying to "travel through time." He was taken to a local hospital where he remains in stable condition, with pending charges of reckless driving.

Florida Man Arrested After Walking Out of Store with AK-47s Stuffed Down His Pants

FT. LAUDERDALE — A Florida man faces grand theft charges for allegedly trying to steal assault rifles from a pawn shop by stuffing them down his pants.

According to an arrest report, the 19-year-old suspect was seen by the store owner taking an AK-47 from a display rack and stuffing it down his pants. He then took another rifle from another display, and shoved it down his pants before limping out the door. The owner confronted the suspect, and notified police. He was charged with grand theft and violation of a domestic violence injunction.

Florida Man Arrested Trying to Sell Live Iguanas Hog-Tied to His Bicycle

KEY WEST — A Florida line cook was arrested for trying to sell live iguanas that he'd hog-tied to his bicycle, police say. The 35-year-old acquired the animals from a local golf club and strapped them to his handlebars with duct tape and wire. He then tried to sell the lizards to passersby, advertising them as a delicious dinner. A concerned citizen notified police. The suspect told police he only tried peddling the critters to a woman after she wouldn't leave him alone.

Florida Man Arrested After Driving 110 MPH While Naked With 3 Women in a Cadillac

A search of the naked driver's vehicle uncovered empty beer and whiskey bottles

NAPLES — A naked Florida man accused of driving 110 mph with three female passengers was arrested Saturday afternoon on a DUI charge, the Florida Highway Patrol reported.

Authorities responded to a tip of a Cadillac driving recklessly at high speeds heading west towards Naples. An FHP officer spotted the car, which registered 109 mph on his radar, and initiated a traffic stop. The trooper immediately noticed an open 12-pack of beer next to the driver's seat and a shirtless driver.

When the 33-year-old suspect was ordered to step out of the car, the trooper saw he was naked. The man slurred his speech and smelled of alcohol, nearly falling down when attempting to put his pants on.

A search of the vehicle uncovered nearly empty beer bottles and a nearly empty bottle of whiskey. The suspect refused a field sobriety test, and was charged with DUI and misdemeanor driving without a license.

Florida Man Devoured By Alligator While Hiding from Police

"I would say it's poetic justice," a local man surmised.

BREVARD COUNTY — The remains of a would-be burglar were recovered from the stomach of an alligator, according to local news report.

The misfortune started when the suspect and an accomplice were reported wandering behind homes, say neighbors who called police to report the suspicious activity. A manhunt ensued, but the suspects managed to get away. What happens next is not clear, but officers speculate one of the men went to Barefoot Bay Pond to hide from police. His body was found floating in the lake ten days after he was reported missing, with wounds consistent with an alligator attack. When divers attempted to retrieve the body, they were repeatedly attacked by the alligator.

A trapper with Florida Fish and Wildlife was then hired to detain and euthanize the alligator. An analysis of its stomach contents confirmed that the alligator drowned the man and ate a portion of his remains.

"I would say it's poetic justice, you want to sit there and steal from people," a local man surmised.

Florida Woman Smokes Meth, Burns Down Florida's Oldest Tree

Aspiring model lit a fire under the tree so she could see the drugs she was trying to smoke

SEMINOLE COUNTY — An aspiring meth-addicted Florida model was arrested in connection with burning down a 18-foot, 3,500-year-old bald cypress tree in Longwood, Florida. "The Senator," as the tree is known, was not only the state's oldest tree, and the fifth oldest tree in the whole country, but also the largest tree of any type east of the Mississippi.

Claiming on her personal web page to be a nature enthusiast, the 26-year-old woman regularly visited the tree to get high on meth. At around 5:30 am on the morning in question, she lit a fire under the tree so she could see the drugs she planned to smoke.

The suspect later told police that the fire got out of control, and within hours the tree burned to the ground.

She fled the scene after taking several photos and videos of the fire on her phone, which were later recovered. Authorities initially had no leads in the case, but the suspect told several friends about the fire, and one of them tipped off police.

A search of her apartment uncovered meth and drug paraphernalia.

The woman pleaded no contest to unlawful burning of lands, possession of methamphetamine and possession of drug paraphernalia. She admitted to being a methamphetamine addict, and said she had already begun attending drug counseling as a condition of her probation.

Florida Reptile Store Owner Put Lizard in Mouth, Smacked Employees with Critter in Attack

Reptile store owner said to have a taste for the unusual

BROWARD COUNTY — A Florida man was arrested and charged with cruelty to animals after allegedly put a bearded dragon lizard in his mouth and attacked employees with it. The incident was caught on surveillance video, as the suspect can be seen wielding the lizard, smacking employees with its tail, and even throwing Gatorade on the workers. The condition of the lizard is unknown.

The same 40-year-old reptile store owner made national news after a man died during a 2012 insect-eating contest at his establishment. A contestant choked and died while gobbling dozens of roaches and worms in an effort to secure the grand prize, a ball python.

Florida Man Steals Two TVs and a Car from Dealership, Drives Through Double Glass Doors Into Another Car

The thief had no recollection of driving SUV off showroom floor and through glass doors

OCALA — A Florida man was arrested after police responded to reports of a hit-and-run involving a 2014 Toyota 4-Runner. The driver faces charges of grand theft and commercial burglary. He told police he had no recollection of the incident.

Authorities say the suspect removed two large screen television sets from the dealership, placed them in a SUV on the showroom floor, drove through double glass doors into another vehicle before abandoning the SUV at the entrance of a nearby subdivision.

Police found the crashed SUV parked outside the gates of the subdivision with its hazard lights flashing. They noticed the automobile had stickers indicating it came from a local car dealer. They saw the suspect standing next to the car, intoxicated, with a bottle of Aleve in his hand. When it was discovered there were outstanding warrants for his arrest, he was detained. Police say he was first taken to a hospital for an evaluation but became aggressive and was taken instead to the jail.

While he denied recollection of the incident, he admitted an addiction to methamphetamine and pain pills.

Wanted Florida Man Arrested After Butt-Dialing 911

LAKE HAMILTON — A 21-year-old Florida man with an outstanding warrant is under arrest after he pocket-dialed authorities from his cell phone in the early evening. Though the suspect hung up the phone, the call was traced to a local park. Deputies found the man in the park, which had been closed for the evening. When confronted, the suspect became uncooperative. A initial investigation found marijuana in his possession and an outstanding warrant for aggravated battery. He was arrested and charged with failure to appear on an aggravated battery charge, resisting an officer, and possession of marijuana.

Florida Man Too Drunk to Be Honored by Mothers Against Drunk Driving

PINELLAS COUNTY — A Florida police officer attending an anti-drunk driving conference in which he was scheduled to receive an award for making over 100 DUI arrests was too drunk to collect his prize. Reports allege the cop drank all or part of a bottle of whiskey while driving to the event in his police cruiser. Once he arrived, he skipped several educational sessions to drink and play games in the hotel courtyard. One witness describes seeing the man stumbling around the hotel hallways in his underwear. When confronted, the cop said he only had one or two drinks.

Florida Man Bit by Shark Catches Shark, Says He'll Eat It

Man returns to scene of attack, intent to smoke and eat the fish

JUPITER — A Florida man is lucky to be alive after an encounter with a shark off Singer Island. The shark bit his hand and tried to pull him underwater.

"I was pulling my left hand out of the water and as it was coming out of the water, he jerked it back down," he said about the shark. "I could feel his nose against my skin. I'm wrestling him and he's trying to pull me down," he continued. The shark released and he was able to make it back to shore. The bite was treated with 15 stitches at a local hospital.

But the story didn't end there. The 28-year-old Jupiter resident, a commercial fisherman, returned to the scene of the attack early the next week with a friend.

Unable to fish himself due to the injury, he was overjoyed when a friend hooked what he believed to be the same shark and reeled him in. A bystander with young kids asked him to return the shark to the water, but the wounded man was intent on smoking and eating it.

"Now that we got the shark that bit my hand, we're going to fillet him and eat him," he said.

Florida Man Arrested With 'Go Directly to Jail' Monopoly Shirt On

Florida Man Steals Chainsaw By Shoving It Down His Pants, Flees On Bicycle

LEE COUNTY — A Florida man arrested for possession of marijuana and drug paraphernalia was released after posting $6,500 bail, according to the Lee County Sheriff's Department. He was shown in a mugshot wearing a green T-shirt with the Monopoly board game slogan, "Go Directly to Jail." It is unknown whether he has an attorney.

PORT LUCIE — A Florida man walked into a local lawn equipment store and perused the equipment before asking the cashier for change. While the cashier was distracted, he shoved a chainsaw down his pants and fled on a bicycle. The heist was witnessed by store employees who chased the shoplifter, prompting him to ditch the power tool in a wooded area. He was arrested a short time later. The device vas off at the time.

Armed Florida Men Attack Ice Cream Man

OCALA — An ice cream man said three armed gunmen attacked him after they tried to give him a counterfeit $20 bill. The victim told police the men tried to pay for a pickled sausage with a counterfeit $20 bill. When the ice cream man confronted them, they pulled a gun. A tussle ensued, and the ice cream man was struck in the eye. The suspects fled in a 1980s model Cadillac. They are still at large.

Florida Man, 81, Attacks Rival Over Shuffleboard

PINELLAS COUNTY — An 81-year-old Florida man allegedly lost his temper and attacked a fellow senior citizen over a game of shuffleboard. The two men were residents of Pinellas Park Seniors Center. On the day of the attack, the two were involved in a disagreement over the outcome of a shuffleboard game. The disgruntled 81-year-old attacker punched the victim in the face and then slammed him with the shuffleboard cue. The victim was treated and released from a local hospital, while the attacker was charged with misdemeanor battery.

Florida Man Poses as Police Officer to Get Free Meal at IHOP, Moons Employee

Prior to arrest, suspect exclaimed, "I'm a Green Beret! If I die, Obama dies!"

ORLANDO — A Florida man allegedly posed as a police officer to get a free meal at IHOP and then flashed his buttocks at a server when he was refused service.

The 55-year-old man arrived at a local IHOP at 1 a.m., telling the server, "I am a cop and I get food for free." He then produced a patch with police insignia as identification. When the server responded that police officers do, in fact, pay for their meals, the man refused to leave until he was fed. He then pulled down his pants and flashed his buttocks to the IHOP staff, threatening violence.

When police arrived at the scene to arrest him, the suspect proclaimed, "I'm a Green Beret! If I die, Obama dies!" He also bragged about his close ties to the Orlando Police Department.

He was detained on charges of impersonating a law enforcement officer, trespassing and disorderly conduct. The restaurant manager told police he recognized the man from a prior encounter in which he did not have money to pay for his meal.

Florida Man Arrested in Argument Over Noodles

Florida Man Arrested for Smoking Pot in Maternity Ward After Delivery

GAINESVILLE — Gainesville Police arrested a local man after he assaulted his nephew during an argument over undercooked noodles. According to police reports, the 54-year-old suspect told his nephew the noodles he prepared were undercooked. A minor altercation ensued, at which point the nephew fled to a nearby apartment. The assailant followed him there, continuing to yell obscenities and threaten him. The suspect rushed towards him with a knife while making slashing motions, the report states. He was charged with aggravated assault and domestic battery.

STUART — A nurse in the infant delivery unit at a local hospital alerted police that she smelled marijuana coming from a man whose girlfriend was admitted after delivering a child. The officer who arrived on the scene asked the suspect to handover the cannibis. The new father reached in his pocket and handed over a pipe-like device that contained marijuana. He was arrested and charged with possession of marijuana and drug paraphernalia.

Florida Man Buries Boss Waist Deep in Dirt Using a Front Loader

Machine operator, known as "Pork Chop," claims the incident was an accident

VOLUSIA COUNTY — A 32-year-old Sanford man was arrested for burying his boss up to the waist, according to an arrest report. The man, who goes by "Pork Chop," began arguing with his boss at the construction site of a new WalMart in the early morning. According to witnesses, he then dumped a load of dirt on the head of the 52-year-old superintendent, pinning him to the ground. He then dumped another dirt load, covering the man up to his waist.

That's when things went from bad to worse. According to eyewitness reports, Pork Chop got out of the front-end loader, picked up a 6 foot aluminum tool and began whacking his boss in the head.

He then started cursing and laughing before some other coworkers showed up to help excavate the pinned boss.

Pork Chop told a different version of events. He claimed his boss verbally abused him and threatened physical violence that morning. He said he "accidentally" buried him when his leg inadvertently hit the control gear of the front-loader.

Authorities were not impressed, and arrested him on charges of aggravated battery. Records show the man has a criminal history with aggravated battery and domestic violence convictions.

Man Kills Imaginary Friend, Turns Self In

Man describes gruesome murder of "Mr. Happy," threatens violence when not offered the death penalty

JACKSONVILLE — A Florida man walked into the Jacksonville Sheriff's Office and told deputies he had a confession to make. The man claimed he murdered his friend, "Mr. Happy," with a kitchen knife, cut him up with a hatchet, and buried the remains in his backyard.

The motive behind the attack are best described in his own words: "He left his empty vodka bottles all over the kitchen... never picked up his empty cocaine baggies...He messed up my apartment to the point where I just couldn't get it clean... Before Hap started doing drugs and acting weird he was my BFF... We'd go dancing, play on the children's park equipment, both huge fans of doom metal and listened to it for hours with the lights turned off."

The man also claimed he was framed for a drunk driving incident in which Mr. Happy crashed his car.

"That drunk driving incident I got unfairly blamed for and just how messy he had become put me over the edge and I murdered him."

Mr. Happy, it turns out, was his imaginary friend. The man was arrested and threatened violence when he was not offered the death penalty. A search of his home uncovered drug paraphernalia and a ᴜachine gun.

Florida Man Waves American Flag, Blasts Slayer During Hurricane Matthew

Florida Man Shoots Self, Realizes it Three Days Later

JACKSONVILLE — A video released just after Hurricane Matthew ravaged northeast Florida shows a local man challenging the hurricane by standing in the street of a Jacksonville Beach neighborhood in hurricane force winds waving an American flag and jamming to heavy metal music. The video shows the man confidently standing in the street with his hair whipping around while waving the flag to "Raining Blood" by heavy metal band Slayer. He said in the video's description that he "had a request for some hair action during the 'cane."

DELTONA — A Florida man checked into a local hospital after realizing that he shot himself three days ago. The 37-year-old claimed he was cleaning his .22 caliber pistol in his living room, holding the weapon close to his chest so his dog would not interfere. At some point the weapon discharged and he fell face down on the floor. The man said he did not feel any pain on account of the pain medications he takes for back problems. He reportedly continued about his normal routines for the next two days, when he noticed a blood stain on the black long-sleeved shirt he had worn since the incident. He removed the shirt and noticed a bullet hole in his arm, so he drove himself to the hospital for treatment. No charges were filed.

Florida Man Eats Own Fingers to Avoid Being Fingerprinted

LEE COUNTY — A Florida man arrested for theft of a Mercedes chewed off and ate his fingertips to avoid being fingerprinted by police. The 20-year-old suspect is seen in surveillance footage gnawing his fingers, chewing and then swallowing as he sat in the back of a patrol car. Despite the self-mutilation, a fingertip scanner was able to identify the suspect, who was also found to be carrying a fake I.D., three fake credit cards and a firearm. The motive appears to be an outstanding warrant for aggravated assault with a deadly weapon.

Florida Man Blows Off Arms Making Fireworks With Coffee Grinder

CAPE CORAL — No charges were filed in the case of a Florida man who used a coffee grinder in his kitchen to mix explosive materials, authorities say. The 31-year-old's limbs were blown off below the elbows when the mixture exploded. He was taken to a local hospital for emergency surgery. Prosecutors intended to charge the man with manufacturing and discharging a destructive device, but later decided the incident did not represent criminal intent. Investigators speculate the concoction exploded when he accidentally knocked the coffee grinder down. His condition is not known.

Drunk Florida Man Tries to Use Taco as ID After His Car Catches Fire at Taco Bell

After falling asleep at the drive-thru window, truck catches fire and man produces taco as identification

JENSEN BEACH — A Florida man arrived at a local Taco Bell in the early morning hours after having a few beers. He placed his ordered and then fell asleep in his truck after being served. The store manager alerted authorities, as the man was fast-asleep at the drive-thru window while other customers were waiting in line. Asked for identification, the 31-year-old handed them a taco. When the officer clarified that a taco is not a legal form of identification, the man chuckled and ate the taco.

Deputies additionally noted that the man had fallen asleep with his foot on the accelerator while his truck was in park. This caused the engine to catch fire, and fire crews had to be called to extinguish it. His blood alcohol was three times the legal limit, and he was arrested on DUI charges.

Florida Man Arrested After Cop Mistakes Krispy Kreme Doughnut Glaze for Meth

Speculation as to why Krispy Kreme doughnuts are so addictive ensues

ORLANDO — A Florida man filed a lawsuit against the city of Orlando after he was arrested, jailed, and strip-searched after being charged with possession of methamphetamine.

The 64-year-old was pulled over for speeding while driving an elderly friend home from work. When the officer asked for identification, the man opened his wallet, showing a concealed carry permit. He revealed that he was carrying a weapon, and was asked to step out of the car. The officer said she spotted "a rock like substance on the floor board where his feet were."

"I recognized through my eleven years of training and experience as a law enforcement officer the substance to be some sort of narcotic," the veteran officer stated in the arrest report.

A field test reportedly tested positive for amphetamines. The suspect said he had never done drugs in his life, and "the substance is sugar from a Krispy Kreme doughnut" that he ate. A follow up test from the crime lab was negative, exonerating the man six weeks after the arrest. But police stood by their claims, stating the arrest was a legitimate one, and that false positives with field testing are known to occur. He is seeking unspecified damages.

Tar-Covered Florida Man Arrested on Gas Station Roof

Florida Man Arrested for Hacking ATM with Hatchet

DAYTONA BEACH — Police responded to a call at a gas station to find a man covered tar standing on the roof just before sunrise. The 30-year-old local man first told authorities he was visiting family. When the officers didn't believe him, he then claimed he was a repairman who climbed the roof to investigate a noise air-conditioner. Finally, police say, he told them he was sleeping on the roof and smothered himself in tar so he wouldn't be discovered. A search recovered a prying tool police believe he intended to use in a burglary. He was charged with attempted burglary of an unoccupied structure, possession of burglary tools and criminal mischief.

DAYTONA BEACH — A central Florida man was seen on surveillance video using a hatchet to open an ATM. Police say he used the hatchet to open the machine, but no money was stolen. He was arrested a short time later, and charged with burglary and criminal mischief with damage to property. The ATM machine sustained $1000 worth of damage in the attack.

Florida Man Dances on Patrol Car Roof to Save Children from Vampires

Suspect was arrested in April after he struck the back of a patrol vehicle, danced on the roof, broke the windshield wipers and took an American Flag from a neighbor's yard

LEE COUNTY — A Florida man was caught on surveillance video crashing his car in to the bumper of a marked police cruiser parked at a private residence. The 44-year-old Cape Coral man then climbed on the roof of the patrol car and danced for six minutes to Hall & Oates' "Rich Girl" and Supertramp's "Goodbye Stranger." When he finished, he ripped off a windshield wiper, tossed it away, and returned with an American flag he stole from a neighbor's yard. The convicted sex offender wandered around a bit more, before deputies arrived and arrested him.

While being taken into custody, the man is heard singing an encore from the musical, "Grease." His explanation: a woman with fangs was threatening him, and a human sacrifice was about to occur involving vampires. He was charged with criminal mischief and disturbing the peace.

Naked Florida Man Arrested After Flashing Passersby with Electrical Device Attached to Penis

Local man arrested when victim refused invitation into vehicle, takes photo with mobile device

BOYNTON BEACH — A Florida man has been arrested after attaching electrical wires to his penis and flashing his genitals to passersby while driving around a gated community.

The naked 56-year-old attached a 'muscle stimulator' device to his genitals and slowed his white Toyota to show pedestrians the device before inviting them to join him in the car. An offended witness declined the invitation, and phoned police after taking a photograph of the man with a mobile phone. In the photograph, the suspect is seen sitting naked in the drivers seat with his seatbelt fastened and electrical wires attached to his genitalia. A remote control to the device is seen next to his gear stick.

According to police, "The victim advised he observed a naked man driving a white 4 door Toyota slowly through his neighborhood. As the subject drove by the victim he gestured at the victim to look down towards his groin area where the victim observed an electronic device with wires attached to [his] penis. The victim advised he turned down the advances and contacted our agency."

The official police report states that prior to being apprehended, the man continued driving towards a school and slowed down, but did not make contact with any of the children. He is later seen in a mugshot with multiple bruises and lacerations to his face, injuries that resulted from a scuffle with police while resisting arrest. He was charged with lewd and lascivious exhibition, exposure of sexual organs and resisting a law enforcement officer without violence.

Florida Man Arrested for Flashing Drive-Thru Workers

HAYWARD — A Florida man suspected in a string of serial flashing at a local McDonalds is now under arrest after a police sting. The 57-year-old suspect, a convicted sex offender, was arrested on charges of indecent exposure after flashing his genitals to female employees of a local McDonalds restaurant.

The first reported flashing occurred when the man pulled into the drive-thru, ordered food, but instead of paying he exposed himself to the cashier. He drove away after the employee shut the window. A week later, a similar incident occurred at the same restaurant. Again, the man drove away before police arrived.

Two weeks later, police secretly staked out the restaurant. When employees noticed the man in his blue SUV pull into the drive-thru again, they alerted police who quickly moved in and blocked his car with a police cruiser. He stepped out his his vehicle, and authorities noted his genitals exposed through a hole cut in the crotch of his pants. He was arrested on suspicion of indecent exposure.

Florida Man Accused of Making Meth in Public Restroom

Florida Man Stole 850 Pairs of Underwear From Victoria's Secret

NEW SMYRNA BEACH — A Florida man was arrested after allegedly trying to set up a meth lab in the restroom of a local park. A construction worker notified police of a strange smelling smoke seeping from under the door and out of the windows of a men's bathroom in the park. When police arrived, they found remnants of a meth lab, and saw the man running away with a bag in his hand. Then 20-year-old suspect was apprehended a short time later. Records show he is also a suspect in a home burglary.

BROWARD COUNTY — A Florida man was arrested for stealing 850 pairs of underwear from Victoria's Secret. The thefts occurred over three trips to the women's lingerie store. One one occasion, the suspect stole 300 pairs of underwear; on another date, 175 pairs of women's underwear; and in a final heist, stole 375 pairs of underwear. The total value of the thefts exceeds $15,000, police say. The suspect is a recent high school graduate who lives with his parents. "Thank you," the judge said at the hearing. "Don't come back to Victoria's Secret."

Florida Man Harassing Restaurants Banned from Pizza Delivery

Suspect led delivery personnel to fake addresses, called back to say the pizza was gross

SEBASTIAN — A Florida man was banned from pizza delivery after harassing local restaurants, authorities say. Police say that over a three week period the man made orders over the telephone, but refused to pay for them, misdirected delivery personnel to fake addresses, or called to complain about the taste of the pizza. In some cases he used a fake name, or placed his orders using various phone numbers. At his arraignment, the judge ordered the man never again call for pizza delivery: "Defendant shall refrain from calling any pizza establishment and/or making any harassing calls or his bond shall be revoked," the warrant affidavit states.

Records show he faced similar charges of harassing phone calls eight years prior. He was charged with four counts of harassing phone calls, two counts of first-degree petty theft and one count of second-degree petty theft for the $667 of lost income the restaurants incurred.

Florida Man Overcomes Fear of Spiders By Tattooing Spider on His Face

Florida Man Bites Neighbor's Ear Off Over a Cigarette

DELTONA — A Florida man decided to face his fear of spiders by tattooing a black widow on his cheek.

"Everybody fears spiders," the 24-year-old Deltona resident told a local newspaper. "That's why I got it. Just to, like, make me know, that that's what I fear, but not to fear it. You know what I'm saying?"

He continued, "Some people say 'Why did you get it? You're never going to get a job,'" he said. "Some people say 'It's cool, man. The tattoo on the face, I would never get it but that one came out cool.'"

The arachnophobic man posted pictures of the tattoo on Facebook, obviously proud of the artwork. His girlfriend was not impressed, however, and he soon changed his relationship status to 'single.'

PALM BEACH — A Florida man inspired by Mike Tyson bit his neighbor's ear off because he didn't give him a cigarette.

According to police, the victim had a chunk of his ear bitten off in a brutal attack after he refused to give the man a smoke. The victim told police he was helping a friend when the suspect, his neighbor, asked if could bum a smoke. After refusing, the attacker faked giving the victim a bear hug before chomping down on his ear.

"I was helping a friend out and someone decided they wanted to take a chunk out of my ear... This all started because I wouldn't give him a cigarette," the victim said.

Florida Man Offers Police Chicken Dinner and $3 for Sex Act

Florida Man Arrested on Bicycle in Drive-Thru Lane of Taco Bell

SANFORD — Seven men are under arrest after prostitution sting in which a female officer posed as a street level prostitute as part of an ongoing investigation. During the decoy operation, one of the suspects offered to trade $3 and a chicken dinner for a sexual act, police say.

DAYTONA BEACH — A Florida man was refused service at Taco Bell because he was on a bicycle in the drive-thru lane.

The 33-year-old intoxicated central Florida man arrived on bicycle just after 3 a.m. when the restaurant was closing. He was refused service but refused to leave, prompting calls to police. Deputies arrived to find the suspect still sitting on his bicycle at the ordering speaker. Again the man refused to leave, and tussled with police after they noticed a Swiss Army knife on his belt. He was wrestled to the ground and arrested with charges of resisting arrest with violence. He was later released.

Florida Man in Boy Scout Uniform Arrested for Resisting Officer on Halloween

Man dressed as Boy Scout found intoxicated, slumped in convertible on Halloween

ORANGE COUNTY — A Florida man is behind bars after resisting arrest without violence, news outlets report. When police spotted a vehicle parked facing the wrong direction in the early morning hours after Halloween, they found the 24-year-old dressed as boy scout, slumped over in the driver's seat of his convertible. When police approached the suspect, he initially denied that his vehicle was improperly faced. He then refused to produce a driver's license, but removed it from his wallet under the threat of arrest, only to refuse handing it over. He eventually handed the license over, but then refused to exit the vehicle.

Police noticed he had blood shot eyes and smelled of alcohol, so they physically removed him from the vehicle and arrested him. A field sobriety test was not performed due to his "uncooperative nature," police said. The series of events leading to his predicament are not known.

Florida Man Steals Truck with 36,000 Pounds of Crisco Inside

ST. PETERSBURG — A group of men stole a semitrailer truck bound for a Publix distribution center with 36,000 pounds of Crisco sticks inside, police report. The truck was parked at the time of the theft and was found abandoned several days later. It is not immediately known if the 36,000 pounds of the vegetable shortening was still inside. The suspects are still at large.

Identical Twin Florida Men Arrested After Getting in Brick Fight

ORANGE CITY — A pair of identical Florida twins were arrested after they began throwing bricks at each other, police said. The 52-year-old men became involved in an argument in the front yard when one threatened to throw a brick at his brother. The brother grabbed a similar sized brick to defend himself. The threats turned to violence when both starting hurling the bricks at one another. When police arrived, the men were arrested and charged with identical counts of aggravated battery. One man suffered minor damage to his eye; his brother was struck in the leg.

Florida Man Steals $2 Million in Legos

Authorities say the suspect's mother was also involved, acted as a lookout

DUPAGE COUNTY — Authorities say a Florida man made over $1 million selling Legos and other stolen goods online. The 49-year-old is accused of stealing over $2 million worth of legos in all 50 states from Toys 'R' Us stores, using the proceeds to finance a lavish lifestyle. He was eventually caught after becoming dependent on a Toys 'R' Us rewards card and served jail time.

While on probation after his release, he told his parole officer he intended to travel to Illinois to visit relatives. Knowing the man had no relatives in Illinois, authorities set up a sting.

Undercover detectives attached a monitoring device to his vehicle and followed him around town. They watched patiently for several days as he lingered around department stores, staying in hotels nearby. When probable cause was sufficient, they executed a search and recovered numerous goods stolen from nearby stores. At his hearing, a judge ordered that he wear an ankle monitor after being released from prison. The lego thief responded, "Having an ankle monitor would be beautiful. I could stay home and take care of my mother, who's in hospice."

Florida Man Sought in Theft of $300 Jenna Jameson Sex Doll

VERO BEACH — Police are searching for an "unidentified white male" who fled from an adult novelty store with a $300 Jenna Jameson sex doll in tow. The suspect walked up to the counter to ask some questions about the doll. He then grabbed the doll and ran. Both the thief and the battery-powered doll are at large.

Florida Man Smokes Crack in Hospital ICU, Starts Fire

OKALOOSA — A fire was started in the intensive care unit of a local hospital after a patient in the unit smoked crack cocaine allegedly supplied by a friend on Christmas Eve. Police say a 54-year-old local man showed up to the hospital to visit his ailing friend, and brought him crack cocaine, a smoking device, and a loaded firearm. When the patient lit up, the tubing that supplied him oxygen caught on fire. The fire was promptly extinguished, and damages were minimal. The patient's friend was arrested on several charges.

Florida Man on Drug-Induced Naked Rampage Bites Girlfriend

The naked man destroyed items in home while screaming everyone was doing to die

PALM BEACH COUNTY — An 18-year-old Jupiter man high on LSD was arrested after going on a naked rampage inside a house while screaming that everyone was going to die.

Police responded to a call of domestic disturbance, and when they arrived the suspect and his girlfriend were acting bizarrely and swinging their arms at each other. When police ordered the male suspect to the ground, he fell backwards, continuing to scream that everyone was going to die. His 17-year-old girlfriend then ran over to him and pointed her finger in the man's face, prompting him to bit down on her finger, causing a laceration. He had to be sedated before being taken into custody.

An eyewitness told police the incident started when the couple began arguing in the backyard. The male suspect tossed the girl around violently before walking into the house, stripping naked, and smashing mirrors and other items. He faces charges of battery, resisting an officer with violence, criminal mischief of $200 or less and child abuse without great bodily harm.

Florida Man on Bath Salts Head-Butts Vehicle, Attacks Fire Official

VOLUSIA COUNTY — A county fire chief suffered minor injuries after a man high on bath salts attacked him after the chief stopped to help a woman whose car was damaged by the suspect.

According to police, the 35-year-old local man dove head first onto the hood of a Kia and head-butted the windshield. The incident caused several dents in the car's body and a crack in the windshield. The driver of the car, and unidentified woman, stopped the vehicle and started screaming. When the fire chief arrived after hearing a call for help, the man was sprawled on the car's hood and did not respond to commands. An altercation ensued, and the suspect slapped the fire chief, prompting the chief to hit the suspect in the face with his portable radio.

Two witnesses at the scene helped detain the suspect until police arrived. The suspect was charged with failure to appear on a retail theft charge, battery on a firefighter and criminal mischief of more than $1,000. He later admitted to having taken methadone and bath salts, deputies said.

Florida Man High on Meth Jumps on Strangers' Cars, Surfs Them

Suspect continues surfing moving vehicle, peering through window at terrified driver

MANALAPAN — Witnesses say a 25-year-old resident of Coral Springs jumped out of his girlfriend's car in the middle of traffic and proceeded to jump onto several cars nearby, including a moving convertible. One witness, who caught the incident on cellphone video, said, "He was running around like a monkey with his tongue out, waving his arms in the air, jumping on top of cars."

The video shows one driver continuing to drive after the suspect jumped on the roof of her Nissan Altima. The suspect is seen kneeling down on the hood of the moving car, even leaning over to peer inside the windows at the driver.

When police approached from the opposite direction, the car-surfing man jumped down and attempted to flee.

"When he went to run away from the cops, he didn't even run away from them," the man who recorded the video said. "He ran a few feet and then ran back at them. He was really confused, just acting crazy. I've never seen anything like it."

The man was detained without incident and faces charges of public intoxication, disorderly conduct and criminal mischief for causing more than $1,000 damage to two different cars. Officers say he admitted to using crystal meth and claimed someone was after him.

82-Year-Old Florida Man Slashes 88-Year-Old Florida Woman's Tires With an Ice Pick for Taking His Seat at Bingo

LAKE WALES — An 82-year-old Florida man was arrested for slashing a woman's tires because he claimed she was sitting in his favorite bingo seat. Police say he took an ice pick to the tires of the 88-year-old victim's car during a weekly bingo game at a local retirement community. According to reports, the man stormed out of the facility, slashing the elderly woman's tires because she was sitting in a chair he usually sits in. The incident was caught on surveillance video, and the man admitted to the crime and expressed regret.

Florida Man Covered in Pizza Arrested for Battery

TREASURE ISLAND — A Florida man on probation was arrested after he threw a hot slice of pizza at his female roommate during a dispute in their apartment. According to police, the 50-year-old Treasure Island resident and his 56-year-old roommate "had an argument about pizza." The nature of the argument is not known. The argument turned violent when the suspect threw a hot slice of pizza on the woman. When police arrived, the suspect, who had pizza sauce on his chest and pants, claimed the woman threw pizza on him. He was charged with simple battery and violating the terms of his probation for a previous drunk driving offense.

Florida Man Dressed as Pirate Arrested for Firing Musket at Passing Cars

The pirate, armed with two muskets and other medieval weaponry, claimed shots were only blanks

MARATHON — A Florida man dressed as a pirate fired two black-powder pistols at cars on a busy bridge, police say. Passersby called police when they witnessed a man wearing pirate regalia and armed with two 18th century muskets and other medieval weaponry including a dagger, knife and sword, firing at passing cars. He told police he was watching the sunset when he decided to fire a couple of rounds. Witnesses say he fired once towards the water, then again at passing cars.

The 56-year-old pirate told police they were only blanks, not live rounds, and that he was an entertainer who dressed as a pirate for parties. He was arrested on charges of disorderly conduct.

Florida Man Steals Operating Room Table from Hospital

Surveillance video shows the man wheeling the table out of the hospital, loading it into a white van before driving off

CLEARWATER — A Florida man walked into a hospital and attempted to flee with a $48,000 operating room table in tow, local media report.

Police say the 52-year-old Clearwater resident gained access to the secure surgical area of a local hospital in the middle of the day. He wheeled an operating table to the back loading dock, where he loaded the table into the back of a white van and drove off, surveillance video shows. The suspect was apprehended several days later on burglary and grand theft charges.

He has prior arrests for aggravated battery and contempt of court, and a conviction for felony grand theft. It is not known if the operating room table was recovered.

350-Pound Florida Man Attempts to Steal 2 TV's from Walmart, Trips after Pants Fall Down

FT. LAUDERDALE — A 350-pound Florida man ran from a Walmart with two stolen TVs in tow, but was apprehended by police after his pants, containing his identification, fell down as he attempted to flee with the merchandise. In a search after the 3:43 A.M arrest, the suspect was also found to have a crack pipe buried in his anus.

According to a police report, the 45-year-old man entered a local Walmart and walked up to a cashier holding two 40-inch televisions. He then bolted before the cashier could scan the merchandise. As he ran through the parking lot with televisions in tow, his pants fell down to his ankles, but he continued running pants-less. The incident was captured on surveillance video.

A search of the man's pants subsequently uncovered a medical identification card, which led to his arrest about a week later. He was transported to the Pinellas County Jail, when he informed officers he had a crack pipe concealed in his anus. The glass pipe was recovered, and found stuffed with steal wool.

The suspect was charged with grand theft and possession of drug paraphernalia. His prior arrests include aggravated battery, robbery, theft, possession of drug paraphernalia, and driving vithout a license.

Florida Man Arrested for Shoplifting to Pay Wife's Bail

Snake Emerges from Car's Hood While Florida Man Driving

WINTER HAVEN — A 48-year-old shoplifting suspect was arrested after stealing three packs of electric wire from a local Walmart, Winter Haven police say. When asked about the motives for his theft, the man explained that he intended to sell it on the street as a means to pay for his wife's bail. She was arrested days before on charges of, you guessed it, shoplifting.

DUNEDIN — A Florida man was driving home on a busy highway one afternoon when, to his surprise, a 6-foot-long snake emerged from under his hood. The snake appeared on his windshield, at which point he immediately pulled into a local Walmart parking lot and recorded the incident on his mobile phone. Video shows the long black snake slithering on his hood and windshield. The man told police that he had visited a local state park over the weekend, where he believes the snake entered his car. The snake escaped and its immediate whereabouts are unknown.

Florida Thieves Abandon Carjacking, Unable to Drive Stick-Shift

Suspects abandon carjacking, foiled by presence of clutch and manual transmission

ORLANDO — An Orlando Corvette owner was approached by two armed men in an attempted car jacking, media outlets report. The car owner was sitting in his yellow Corvette parked outside Orlando Regional Medical Center when the would-be thieves caught him by surprise.

"He started yanking on the door and made me open the door. He kind of flung it open and dragged me out and demanded that I get on the ground... face down, so I couldn't look at him, of course," the 51-year-old victim told local reporters. He said one of the men pointed a gun at him while the other asked how to operate the vehicle.

"I had to tell him four different times to push in the clutch, because it's a standard transmission."

Still unable to figure out the clutch, the men fled the scene. Before fleeing, they took the man's phone, keys, and wallet.

"My first thought was I guess we don't have driver's ed in school anymore because no one knows how to drive a stick," the victim said. "And my second thing was, don't shoot me because you can't start the car. I'm trying to help you out here."

The suspects remained at large at the time of the story.

Florida Man Breaks Into Home, Eats Bologna and Takes a Nap

PASCO COUNTY — A Florida man was arrested after he broke into a house, had a snack, and fell asleep. The 20-year-old suspect was found by police asleep in the bed of the burglarized home. He admitted to entering through an unlocked door, eating bologna, and passing out. The homeowner reported he consumed over $100 in groceries, and that deodorant was missing as well. The suspect was detained on a minor theft charge, but arrest records show previous charges of armed burglary, and grand theft of lawn equipment and guns.

Florida Man Arrested After Stuffing Steak, Lobster in His Pants

BROOKSVILLE — A Florida man is in custody after police say he stole steak and lobster from Walmart, shoving them down his pants. The 57-year-old suspect was observed putting six packages of steak and two packages of lobster down his pants and walking past all cashiers before casually exiting the store. He was immediately taken into custody. The value of the steak and lobsters was approximately $170.

Florida Man Attempts to Steal Yacht, Sinks It

Suspect sinks boat, swims out to sea when police arrive

MIAMI — When the captain of an 80-foot luxury yacht departed the boat after docking at a local marina, police say a Florida man boarded the vessel and tried to take off. The owner of another boat docked nearby was sleeping at the time, but awoke from all the commotion. He witnessed the yacht going forwards and backwards trying to get out of the slip.

"The guy was a freakin' lunatic. I just thank God he didn't crash into my boat, really, I mean I got damage but not as much as there could have been. My life was in jeopardy," he said. Another witness said, "You heard the engine rev all the way up and he hit it forward front on first. Then he reversed and turned around, he backed up into it. He hit the docks, he hit people's boats."

Apparently the boat thief had difficulty steering the yacht because one of the engines had lost power. The series of collisions caused a hole in the boat's hull, causing it to partially sink.

When police arrived, the suspect jumped overboard and began swimming out to sea. Amazingly, he escaped.

Early the next morning, police discovered a second theft attempt of another yacht docked at the same marina, which again was partially sunk. It is not clear if the original suspect was responsible for the second theft attempt. Recovery efforts of the partially sunk $3.2 million dollar yacht were delayed due to impending hurricane Matthew. Much of the incident was caught on video.

Florida Man Wakeboards Through Flooded Ditch While Being Pulled by Horse

PALATKA — A video posted on Facebook is going viral, as it shows a Florida man on a wakeboard being pulled by a horse through a flooded ditch. The horse was ridden by his 20-year-old brother. The display was filmed by a friend in the passenger seat of a car keeping pace with the horse. "Go faster," the teen says when told he was being pulled at a mere 20 mph.

Florida Man Complains About Free Cookie, Robs Subway Restaurant

BROWARD COUNTY — A Florida man who complained about a free cookie at Subway, returned to the restaurant and robbed it, police report. Before the incident, the suspect was given a free cookie due to a long wait time in line. He left the restaurant, but returned 30 minutes later to complain about the cookie. He locked the restaurant's front door, and brandished a gun while demanding cash from the register. The cashier handed over the register drawer, and the suspect fled. The incident was captured on security video, and the suspect is still at large.

Florida Man Wearing Old Scrubs Tries to Steal Drugs From Hospital

Suspect planned to steal drugs for his girlfriend, who waited in parked car with 15-month-old daughter

MIAMI — A couple was arrested after a Florida man entered a hospital where he used to work in an effort to steal drugs, wearing his old scrub uniform. Police were called after the man was seen at the hospital wearing old blue scrubs and carrying a hammer. A security guard confronted the man before police arrived, and he reportedly swung the hammer at the guard. He was wrestled to the ground and police later found vials of the powerful sedatives Fentanyl and Versed in his possession.

The 43-year-old suspect told police he stole the narcotics for his girlfriend, who was spotted in their getaway car in the parking lot with her 15-month-old in the backseat. When police approached the vehicle, she sped off, nearly crashing into a security golf cart before being pulled over. She admitted driving the man to the hospital on several occasions to steal drugs.

The man faces charges of burglary with assault or battery, two counts of possession of a controlled substance with the intent to sell, and child neglect. The woman faces charges of burglary with assault or battery and child neglect.

Wanted Florida Man Uses His Own Wanted Poster as Facebook Profile Picture

Police captain: "If you are wanted by the police, it's probably not a good idea to use the 'Wanted of the Week' poster of yourself as your profile pic."

STUART — It started when police responded to a domestic violence dispute late one Monday night. The suspect, a Florida man, had fled the scene before police arrived, but was identified by the victim as a 42-year-old local man, and his address was given to police. As an investigation into the suspect continued the following day, police discovered he had two outstanding warrants for drug related charges. They then came across his Facebook page, which showed his wanted poster from Citrus County as his profile picture.

They later found the suspect sleeping at his brother's house. When he awoke to get dressed, a bag of weed fell out of his pants pocket. He was arrested in connection with the outstanding warrants, and charges in the domestic violence incident are pending.

"Facebook is a great way to communicate and connect with old friends and family," a police captain wrote on the department's Facebook page. "If you are wanted by the police, it's probably not a good idea to use the 'Wanted of the Week' poster of yourself as your profile pic."

Florida Woman Shoots Self While Using Snapchat

Weapon discharges while woman attempts video selfie

DELTONA — A Florida woman suffered minor injuries after accidentally shooting herself while recording video with the Snapchat app, authorities say. The 22-year-old Deltona woman was recording a video of herself playing with a .40-caliber pistol when the weapon discharged and shot her cellphone which she was holding in her hand. She was treated for lacerations to her fingers and released from a local hospital. The injuries were likely caused by glass from the phone shattering, according to the sheriff's office.

Her aunt, who was in the house at the time, heard the gunshots and took the woman to the hospital. The aunt said she threw the gun out of the car window on the way to the hospital. The gun has not been recovered, and the shooting was determined to be accidental.

Florida Man Tries to Fake Urine Test Using Mountain Dew

Suspect identifies himself to police as "Dumb Ass" after plan fails

PANAMA CITY — Police say a Florida man on probation was caught trying to use Mountain Dew as a substitute for urine during a court-mandated drug test. When the man learned he was required to give a urine specimen for a drug test, he filled a small radiator hose from his car with Mountain Dew he had in the glove box. He thought the Mountain Dew resembled the color of urine closely enough that he would not be caught. But when complying with the test, most of the Mountain Dew spilled from the radiator hose onto his pants, police say.

The man was due in court for a pretrial hearing on charges of trafficking in amphetamine, possession of hydrocodone and paraphernalia, dealing in stolen property, operating a chop shop, towing vehicles with no identifying information, false statements application affidavit regarding lien, and grand theft auto. When confronted with faking the test, he told deputies that his name was "Dumb Ass."

Florida Man Steals Patrol Car, Says 'This is a Felony?'

Florida man casually drives off in police cruiser with lights flashing, wonders if actions were a felony when arrested

DAYTONA BEACH — A Florida man who stole a police cruiser was confused when he was pulled over by police and arrested. The 44-year-old hopped into a parked police car and drove off with the lights flashing. He was driving around town at about 40 mph when police pulled him over and ordered him out of the car. Wearing flip flops, the suspect complied, and immediately offered an apology. He then calmly inquired as to whether his actions were a felony. Patrol car video show the officers laughing in disbelief.

The man was arrested and charged with grand theft with damage more than $1,000, fleeing and attempting to elude, and violation of pre-trial release conditions on a recent drug arrest. An investigation continues as to why the patrol car was left unattended.

Florida Woman Found Talking to a Pack of Cigarettes

Woman claimed to be locked out of home, using free time to practice for a play

PALM BEACH — A Florida woman was arrested after talking to a pack of smokes, police say. A concerned citizen notified police of a woman who appeared to be under the influence of drugs talking to herself. When confronted, the woman said she "was practicing for a play." An arrest report stated the 46-year-old woman was "sweating, her feet were sandy, her pupils very constricted, and her eyes bloodshot." When asked where she lived, she said "she was locked out of her Palm Beach Gardens home and figured she would drive around to practice for her play."

She continued to talk to herself during the interrogation, all along claiming she was practicing for the play again, police said. When it was discovered that the woman had driven over bushes and onto a golf cart path before the incident, police searched her and uncovered six bottles of prescription medications in her purse. She was arrested on a DUI charge.

Florida Man Wields Shotgun, Demands Cell Phone Be Fixed

GAINESVILLE — A Florida man arrived at a local MetroPCS store with a shotgun and demanded his phone be fixed, police say. The store was closed at the time.

The store manager said the 59-year-old man approached the store, yelling obscenities at the manager who told him to wait until the store opened. Enraged, the suspect went back to his car and returned with a shotgun, pointing it at the glass front door. He then told a customer who had just arrived at the store, "You better move, they gonna fix my phone."

He was approached by police after returning to his car without firing shots. Police found that the shotgun was not loaded, but a revolver in the passenger seat was. The suspect, who volunteered that he was being treated for anger management, also threatened police after being arrested. "When I get out, I'm going to kill every one of you," he said. He was taken to the Alachua County jail and charged with aggravated assault and carrying a concealed firearm without a license.

Florida Woman Sells Drugs in McDonald's Drive-Thru

Woman, who asked McDonald's customers if they wanted to buy crack or Xanax, claimed her sister was framing her

PALM BEACH — A Florida woman was arrested attempting to sell drugs in a McDonald's drive-thru lane, deputies say. The 32-year-old woman approached a customer at the end of a drive-thru line at a local McDonalds and asked whether she wanted to buy crack or Xanax. Police were notified and confronted the suspect, who exhibited signed of intoxication, including "slurred speech and swayed as she sat." When asked to hand her purse to police to be searched, she initially claimed the purse was her sister's. Rethinking her story, she then claimed it was her purse, but her sister stole it, and then she took it back.

The purse contained drug paraphernalia, which the woman claimed belonged to her sister who was trying to frame her. She did admit, however, that a straw found in the purse was for the purpose of snorting her prescription of Klonopin. She was arrested on a charge of possession of drug paraphernalia.

Florida Woman Steals Prom Dress, Chainsaw, Head Butts Police Car

Woman steals prom dress and other random items, exhibits bizarre behavior in custody

FREEPORT — A local Florida woman is behind bars after committing a bizarre burglary of her neighbor's home. The neighbor awoke after hearing some commotion in her carport to find the woman escaping with several items stolen from her property. Police were called and recovered an unusual collection of items, including a prom dress, jumper cables, a shovel, an electric leaf blower, a chainsaw, a vanity mirror, two bags of Miracle-Gro, a sling blade, a box fan, and three pecan trees.

On her way to jail, the thief reportedly kicked and head butted the windows and partition of the police cruiser. She also spit on the floor. She was charged with burglary and grand theft.

Florida Woman Who Stole From Walmart Planned to Apply for Job at Walmart

ST. PETERSBURG — A Florida woman turned herself in to police as part of a program known as Operation Safe Surrender, which allows citizens with outstanding warrants for minor crimes to receive leniency in exchange for voluntary surrender. A year prior, she had been caught walking out of a local Walmart with unpaid children's baby items in her cart. She was charged with shoplifting and retail theft, but failed to appear in court to answer the charges.

When the 22-year-old stood before the judge after turning herself in, she was asked of her employment status and future plans.

"I'm looking for [work], I have an interview," she replied. "I'm waiting for Walmart to call me back. I have an interview with them."

The speechless judge remained quiet for 6 seconds, court video shows.

"I'm on 'Candid Camera,' aren't I?" the judge finally replied. "How do you think it's gonna go when the background shows that you tried to take a cart full of stuff from - well - Walmart?" He added, "What do I know? There, I'm over it."

Florida Man Steals Lotto Tickets, Returns to Cash Winning Ticket

PALM BEACH — A Florida man broke into a local convenience store and escaped with $10,000 worth of scratch-off lottery tickets, police say. The suspect was caught on surveillance video entering the store through the ceiling. He went straight to the bin of scratch-off lottery tickets, filling his pockets before wiggling back out through the ceiling.

A short time later, the man attempted to cash a $1000 winning ticket at a nearby store, but the ticket was declined as it had been marked stolen.

The clerk told the man he needed to pose for a photo to be displayed amongst other lottery winners. When he refused, the clerk threatened to call police if he did not allow his photo to be taken. The suspect obliged, and posed for a photograph.

He was arrested a short time later, and the photo was used as evidence against him. He faces charges of burglary, grand theft, and dealing in stolen property.

Made in the USA
Las Vegas, NV
15 November 2023

80887094R00049